The St. Thomas Treaty.

A SERIES OF LETTERS

TO THE

BOSTON DAILY ADVERTISER.

NEW YORK.

1869.

Sutton, Bowne & Co., Printers, 23 Liberty street, New York.

CORRESPONDENCE.

No. 125 Front street,
New York, February 20th, 1869.

To the Editor of the Boston Daily Advertiser:

Dear Sir:—Your valuable paper has of late contained a series of letters from your regular Washington Correspondent, " Dixon," upon the treaty between the United States and Denmark for the purchase of the islands of St. Thomas and St. John, which have been read with great interest by myself and by many of my countrymen, Danes by birth, and citizens of the United States by adoption.

These letters give, so far as we can judge, an impartial and correct, although very condensed, history of the negotiations which led to the conclusion of the treaty; and, being very desirous of having the facts of the case generally known, I beg in behalf of my friends and countrymen, to ask your consent to the reprinting of those letters, for the purpose of having them distributed in the form of a pamphlet.

I am, sir, very respectfully,
your obedient servant,
C. T. CHRISTENSEN.

Office of the Boston Daily Advertiser,
No. 29 Court street, Boston,
February 22d, 1869.

To General C. T. Christensen, New York:

Dear Sir:—We have no objection to the publication which you propose, and shall be very glad if the letters of our correspondent can be made to contribute in any form to the better understanding of an important question.

I remain, sir,
very respectfully, yours,
CHAS. F. DUNBAR.

HISTORY OF THE ST. THOMAS TREATY.

(FROM OUR REGULAR CORRESPONDENT.)

WASHINGTON, January 11, 1869.

What shall be done with the St. Thomas treaty? is one of the most embarrassing questions now before the Senate. Shall it be let alone, rejected, or ratified? Look at the matter as you will, and there are grave difficulties in the way of an adjustment.

The negotiation for the purchase of these Danish islands began a good deal earlier than the public suppose. It goes back to January, 1865—four years ago this month. On the 7th of that month, if I am correct in the date, Mr. Secretary Seward and General Raasloff, the Danish Minister here, met at a Washington dinner party. In the course of the evening, Mr. Seward took General Raasloff aside, and then and there unfolded the idea—saying, I believe, that we wanted the islands for a naval station, and adding that their geographical position made them properly a part of this country.

The Danish Minister, as I hear—and the matter has been a good deal talked about in the closer official circles for some weeks—the Danish Minister was surprised at the proposition, and said that he believed his government would be opposed to selling the islands. Mr. Seward wished it should be brought to the attention of the King of Denmark, remarking that the United States would treat upon the question in a liberal and chivalrous spirit.

The Danish authorities, in due course, responded that the islands were not for sale, and that it was not considered advisable to negotiate on the question. This response reached here early in April, when Mr. Seward was confined to his bed—it will be recalled that he was thrown from his carriage and very seriously hurt. The answer was submitted to Mr. Fred. Seward, acting Secretary of State. He replied that he knew nothing about the matter, and could take no step in relation to it whatever.

This was in Mr. Lincoln's time. I have reason to believe that Mr. Seward had conferred with him, and that the proposal to buy was made with his consent and approval.

General Raasloff was not favorable to the sale. At that time he was merely the King's Minister here, honored alike in private circles and as an official, but not, as he is now, one of the King's confidential advisers. He reported Mr. Seward's illness, and the doubt that was felt as to his recovery—asking, as I understand, for instructions as to his course in the event of the Secretary's death and the appointment of a new man to the State Department. He was advised to let the matter drop, and say nothing more about it till it was again brought forward by the United States.

In April came the assassination of President Lincoln, the assault upon Mr. Seward, and the accession of Mr. Johnson to the Presidency. The war was ended, and all men began preparing for the new order of things. Mr. Seward was long in recovering from the combined effect of the carriage accident and the Payne assault. It was not till in December of that year, 1865, that anything further was said about St. Thomas. A change had taken place in Danish affairs as well as in our own—one ministry had gone out, and there had come in a new ministry, more favorably disposed to Mr. Seward's project than the old one had been.

The general drift of instructions from the new Danish cabinet to the Minister here was, that, while the government had no desire to sell, it was not absolutely unwilling to entertain Mr. Seward's proposition. They said, however, that if the United States wished to buy, the Secretary of State must show his hand and indicate what he was willing to give; if this were done, the King would consider whether or not to enter upon negotiations. This letter came near the end of December, and was communicated at the State Department a day or two before Mr. Seward left for Cuba. The Secretary told General Raasloff that he was going away, might touch at St. Thomas on his return, and would talk further about the purchase when he got back. I hear he gave out that the trip had nothing to do with the project for buying the island. However this was, he saw some of the St. Thomas people during his absence, and appears to have resolved that the purchase must be made.

The situation during the spring of 1866 was a curious one. The King of Denmark did not want to sell—Mr. Seward did want to buy; yet we insisted, with considerable pertinacity, if I am not misinformed, that Denmark should name a price at which she would sell. This, General Raasloff, speaking for his King, refused to do; and no persuasion on the part of Mr. Seward could induce the Danish Government to recede from this position. The project would have here fallen through had it been in the hands of any one less determined than our Secretary. The matter had been talked over more or less in Mr. Johnson's cabinet, and that body favored the purchase. It was inevitable, therefore, that we should take the first step toward reaching the price to be paid, if we got the islands.

In the summer of that year General Raasloff received permission to visit Denmark. On the 18th of July he left here, bearing the following confidential letter, handed to him by Mr. Seward on the day of its date when he called to take leave:

DEPARTMENT OF STATE,
WASHINGTON, July 17, 1866.

SIR:—I have the honor to propose to you that the United States will negotiate with the King of Denmark for the purchase of the Danish Islands in the West Indies, namely, St. Thomas and the adjacent inlets, Santa Cruz and St. John. The United States would be willing to pay for the same five millions of dollars in gold, payable in this country. Negotiation to be by treaty, which, you will of course understand, will require the constitutional ratification of the Senate.

Insomuch as you propose to visit Copenhagen, the United States Minister at that place will be instructed to converse with you or with your government on the subject; but should your government conclude to negotiate, the proceeding will be expected to be conducted here, and not elsewhere.

Accept, sir, the renewed assurance of my high consideration,

WILLIAM H. SEWARD.

This was the beginning of the end—an end yet a long way off from the date of the letter. General Raasloff was a good while in getting home, as Mr. Seward knew he would be before he started. In the fall of 1866 he entered the ministry of the Danish Government as Minister of War to the King. Thereafter the business we had in hand was conducted with Count Frijs, the Minister of Foreign Affairs through Mr. George H. Yeaman, our Minister at Copenhagen, who seems to have entered into Mr. Seward's spirit from the first, and who conducted the negotiation in such a manner as to win from the Secretary warm praise.

I have been thus particular in detailing the initial steps relating to this treaty, in order to show how loath the Danes were to trade, how Mr. Seward had to persuade them into negotiations, how reluctant they were to part with the islands. The subsequent history of the bargain finally made can be told in a few words.

The formal offer of Mr. Seward was, I believe, laid before the Danish cabinet in November, 1866. They seem to have taken it as a part of what we call a game of bluff—they said the proposal "was regarded as *pro forma* only;" that "the terms mentioned are out of the question, as Mr. Seward very well understands;" and that "if it was indicated, even approximately, what sum might be expected, a conclusion could be had much sooner." All this winter, and through the spring of 1867, Mr. Seward was pressing the trade most vigorously. In January, 1867, he telegraphed to Mr. Yeaman, "haste is important." In March he demands: "We want yea or nay, now." In April he complains of the delay, and tells Mr. Yeaman to get an answer "within a short time."

The Danes had a good deal of love for the little colony off our coast. Some members of the ministry were so bitterly opposed to the business that a rupture of the cabinet was threatened. General Raasloff said in March, 1867, "the idea of the sale is an unpleasant thing;" also, that "there are difficulties and objections to be overcome," and that "the smallness of the price offered is an objection to opening negotiations." The relations of Denmark to France and Prussia were on tender footing—these countries were getting ready for war; if hostilities broke out what should Denmark do? It was believed in Copenhagen that England, France and Spain would protest against the sale of the islands, if it became known that Denmark was considering a proposition from us to purchase. The sale would offend those powers—how far could Denmark rely upon the United States if she got into trouble? The correspondence of the early part of 1867 shows most clearly that nothing but Mr. Seward's steady determination could have brought about the treaty. The Danes were more ready any day to drop the business than to go on with it; and it was the middle of May before the combined efforts of Mr. Seward and Mr. Yeaman could bring the Danish Ministry to commit itself to paper—more than two years and four months after we broached the question.

On the 17th of May, 1867, the Danish Minister of Foreign Affairs said the three islands would be sold for fifteen million dollars; St. Thomas and St. John would be sold for ten millions; Santa Cruz for five millions, subject to the approval of France; and the consent of the people of the islands must be had before any transfer could be made. Five months were occupied in reaching a conclusion, and the treaty was signed October 24, 1867. We bought only St. Thomas and St. John—paying therefor seven and a half millions.

The correspondence is voluminous—a great deal of it has never yet been shown outside of the State Department. The noticeable thing in it all is that the Danish government never wanted to sell, and that Mr. Seward never relaxed his purpose to buy. If we did a good thing in getting that treaty, we must thank Mr. Seward heartily, for nothing but his persistence through a period of more than two and a half years overcame the Danish objection to parting with the islands.

Do you say the treaty is a bad thing, and ought to be rejected by the Senate? It is to be remarked that Denmark has been persuaded to ratify it; that the people of the islands have been persuaded to vote for us:—if we reject the treaty, how will it be with Denmark? Will she and the nations of Europe have a right to say our national honor has been violated? This is the question which Mr. Sumner's committee is pondering.

DIXON.

HOW WE MADE THE ST. THOMAS TREATY.

[FROM OUR REGULAR CORRESPONDENT.]

WASHINGTON, January 13, 1869.

In my letter of two days ago I gave the outlines of the history of the St. Thomas treaty. It was signed October 24, 1867, laid before the Senate on the 3d of December following, and has not yet been acted upon, even by Mr. Sumner's committee. The Danish Government claims that this delay is an indignity; that the rejection of the treaty would be a grave discourtesy and a great injustice. Denmark holds that she was persuaded into the sale of the islands against her will by the persistent determination of our Government to get them; and that the course of the negotiation was such as to give her a right now to ask that we shall keep the word pledged in our behalf by the administration.

The question she raises is one that concerns every citizen. If I fully understand the matter, it is not now, as she presents it, for us to so much consider whether we want the islands, as whether we are not already bound in honor to take them.

Mr. Seward's offer of five millions, contained in the transcript sent you two days ago, was made July 17, 1866. In January, 1867, more than two years after we first asked Denmark to sell, Mr. Yeaman, our Minister to Copenhagen, wrote that he had talked with one of the King's Ministers, that "hesitation was felt in the Danish cabinet,'- that "the Danish Government has not yet agreed to treat of the matter" at all. In March of that year he wrote that the Minister of Foreign Affairs "does not feel ready to treat;" that "there is a desire to await the further development of events in Europe;" that the idea of a sale "is an unpleasant thing;" that "some of the cabinet are willing for the matter to be consummated, and others are not;" and that "the smallness of the price is an objection to opening negotiations." On the 30th of April he wrote Mr. Seward a long letter, of which the following is an extract:

"Yesterday evening I had a protracted interview with General Raasloff, the Secretary of War. There had been a cabinet discussion the previous day, and he was expected to communicate to me the views expressed. I learn from him, in substance, that the present cabinet will treat if there can be an agreement upon the terms—that is, the price; though one member is so much opposed he will resign if the matter is effected. . . . I asked him what was the material and specific difficulty felt by the Cabinet in making a communication or an offer on the subject in response to your note of last July. He replied that there was so great a feeling against making a definite offer, against saying *as an offer* that the government would sell for a definite sum, that he did not believe any communication would come in that form. He thought that when it came it would be rather an intimation of a willingness to treat, and an expression of unwillingness to accept the terms offered, and would leave the matter open in that form for renewed proposals from the United States; that if other propositions were made and found acceptable the matter might be accomplished, otherwise not. It is distinctly his opinion that the feeling of the cabinet is that offers must come from the United States, and will not come from Denmark. . . . He said the cabinet felt the great political importance of the cession in its effects upon the the relations of Denmark with other powers, who would consider it as the beginning of the end of their entire colonial system in that quarter, and would regard the act as unkind and unfriendly in Denmark."

For six months Mr. Seward urged every consideration he could advance, calculated to induce Denmark to enter upon the negotiation. One day he writes, "we must have an answer within a short time;" another day he telegraphs, "want yea or nay now." Some of his messages are persuasive, others are peremptory. The President and cabinet back him up; Mr. Yeaman does our work with spirit and intelligence. The Danes could not hold out forever, and the following shows by what steps the agreement as to compensation was reached:

July 17, 1866—Mr. Seward says he will give five millions for the three islands. April 24, 1867—General Raasloff says that this is not more than half enough, and Mr. Yeaman asks the Danes to name their price. May 17—Count Frijs, Minister of Foreign Affairs, offers to sell the three for fifteen millions, or St. Thomas and St. John for en millions, and Santa Cruz for five millions, the sale of the last-named to be subject to the consent of France. May 27—Mr. Seward says he will take the whole lot for seven and a half millions, and "the treaty will be ratified by the United States before a year from this date." June 17—Count Frijs declines this offer, but says he will take that price for St. Thomas and St. John, and half as much for Santa Cruz. To this Mr. Yeaman responds, by order of Mr. Seward, that our offer is withdrawn and the negotiations ended. The Danes showed no regret at this termination of the affair—it was evident that they were not yet seized with any great desire to sell. For three weeks everybody in Copenhagen supposed the matter at an end. But Mr. Seward knew what he was about. Finding that his game of bluff accomplished nothing, he returned to business, and on the 12th of July, Mr. Yeaman, by his direction, closed the trade at seven and a half millions, for St. Thomas and St. John. This was two years and six months after we first offered to buy; a year after we proposed to pay five millions, and fifteen weeks before the treaty was signed.

Denmark, on the 28th of July, 1867, a fortnight after we had said we would take the two islands, wants to know what we are going to do about Santa Cruz, the third. On the 7th of August she renews the inquiry, saying she had made her proposition of May 17th as a whole, though willing to negotiate separately on Santa Cruz as she supposed that the negotiation for the other two islands "was urged forward for reasons of utility to the United States." On the following day Denmark again says, this time in writing, "we consider our proposition as having been accepted as a whole, although the telegraphic answer mentions only that part of it which can and will be immediately acted upon." On the 5th of September she once more expresses a desire to know our determination about this island; and Mr. Yeaman writes that he thinks Frijs and Raasloff "regret" having fixed a separate price on it, and they "*are now acting under a sense of honorable obligation to go forward with the present affair*," that "*they clearly expected the whole proposition to be accepted*," and that "*acting de novo they would not now make the proposition in its present form.*"

Mr. Seward had, after long persuasion, induced the Danes to negotiate—he had got hold of St. Thomas and St. John; now he shows Denmark a new trick and says he believes, on the whole, that he does not want Santa Cruz. On the 23d of September he writes that our proposition "had reference to our situation at the time it was conceived," that now "circumstances seem to have changed," that "we have come to value dollars more and dominion less," and that "the best we can do is to accept the two islands upon the terms which seem to have been agreed upon." Was not that cleverly put? Five days later he assumes a still more lofty air and writes, "if with reference to the present negotiation for the two islands it is necessary or convenient to the Danish government that there shall at the same time be pending a question of an ultimate transfer of a third island, let the Danish government send us a protocol through your legation, to be dealt with, as, on consultation, we shall find practicable and expedient." Where will you find anything better than that? Santa Cruz is utterly ignored—recognized at most in a vague manner under the words " a third island." On the 25th of October, by way of parting, he turns the whole thing off his mind with this:—" If Denmark desires to negotiate for the sale of Santa Cruz, let her make a separate and distinct offer by formal dispatch." That settled Denmark, so far as Santa Cruz was concerned.

If there is any feature in this whole correspondence creditable to us I am not able to find it. It begins with an entreaty and ends with an insult. We beg Denmark to sell us the three islands—when we have got our grasp upon the only one of any value we snub her for presuming to suppose we want the others. Shall we add injury to insult by rejecting the treaty, or will such a rejection be for the general welfare and the glory of our country? These are questions which Mr. Sumner's committee is considering. DIXON.

MR. SEWARD AND THE ST. THOMAS VOTE.

[FROM OUR REGULAR CORRESPONDENT.]

WASHINGTON, Jan. 18, 1869.

In this St. Thomas correspondence there is nothing more worthy our attention than that part which relates to the taking of the vote of the people of the islands upon the question of a transfer to the United States. What was said on this question would fill three or four columns of the *Advertiser*—perhaps I can give you the pith of the matter in single letter.

It was January, 1865, when Mr. Seward made his first proposal to buy the islands. It was May 17, 1867, when the Danish government consented to open negotiations. At that date Count Frijs, the Minister of Foreign Affairs, said, in the event of a cession of the islands " the ratification by the Rigsdag is constitutionally necessary; and, after that, the Danish government will require that the consent of the people of the islands shall be had." On the 27th of May Mr. Seward wrote, " it is not believed that the consent of the people of the islands is necessary." He said they might become citizens of our country, might withdraw from the islands, or might remain under the protection of the United States. These two letters made up the issue, upon which many pages were written during the next five months.

Early in June Mr. Seward wrote that he would allow the people to " reserve their allegiance for two years," and this concession Mr. Yeaman, in announcing it, said he hoped " would be acceptable to the Danish government, and that there might be no occasion for a canvass and an election." On the 6th of the month Mr. Seward telegraphs to Mr. Yeaman, " Denmark may take a vote at her own cost before, not after, she ratifies." On the 16th Mr. Yeaman has an official interview with Count Frijs and General Raasloff, and reports the Count as follows:—

"Finally, as to the consent of the people of the islands, he expressed the conviction of himself and his government that it could not be dispensed with. He thought no difficulty or obstruction would result from it, and said there should be no unnecessary delay in taking the sense of the people. But there were two reasons why, upon mature reflection, the government could not dispense with it. The modern custom in Europe on that subject was so uniform as to amount almost to a rule of public law, and any departure from it would attract marked attention and comment, if not discontent. In addition to this, the people and the government of Denmark were just at this moment intensely interested in the subject of a vote of the people of North Schleswig, under a provision of the treaty of Prague, to determine for themselves their final and permanent relations with Denmark; and though the two cases were not similar in their facts, they were similar in the importance supposed properly to belong to an expression of their wishes by the people of any district and country upon the question of dissolving their former political relations and ties, and assuming or passing under new ones; and that Denmark might find it an impediment, or at least an unpleasant attitude before the world, to alienate one province without the consent of the people, while naturally and so justly desirous that the people of another district should proceed to give an expression of their preferences, and while hoping for such happy results from that expression."

On the 12th of July Mr. Yeaman writes a long letter, saying he has had two interviews with the Danish authorities:—"I urged very earnestly that the vote in the islands should be dispensed with," but "the Count desired a day or two to think of the matter." Mr. Yeaman continues:

"I have lost no opportunity to impress upon the Ministers in the most earnest and explicit manner, the very great preference of myself and my government that the cession shall be absolute and not subject to further conditions; that it cannot be in accordance with the interests or the feelings of either government that the matter should fail after a treaty has been signed; and that nothing should be done that would invite or present an opportunity for the interference and counter-influence in the islands, of those three great powers (England, France, and Spain) which would much rather see the matter fail than succeed; and I have indicated that I am not authorized to agree to such a proposal, and that for me to do so might jeopard the treaty at Washington as well as in the islands. To this it is replied that there is no real danger of failure; that but little time will be allowed for foreign interference or influence upon the election; that ratification by the Rigsdag will be much more sure and easy if the treaty is first voted for by the islands; and the effect of a contrary course upon the Schleswig question as heretofore urged, is now repeated with increased emphasis and earnestness. The cabinet may be brought to give up the vote, but in my opinion it will not be waived. This leaves me in great embarassment, and I have telegraphed you for instructions. But I have resolved that if, without further instructions, it comes to be *a question of taking the treaty with a vote, or not at all, I will yield, it being the only chance left for success.* I will press my objections as far as can well be done this side the point of breaking the negotiations."

To the request for instructions, Mr. Seward, on the 12th of July, answers, "do not agree to submit the question." He finds cause, shortly however, for changing his mind, and on the 7th of August writes in hearty approval of Mr. Yeaman's letter of the 12th of July, above quoted—thus saying, in effect, that at the last moment, *rather than give up the treaty, we would consent to the vote.* The Danes insisted on this condition from first to last, and finally carried their point.

Early in August three new questions came to the front—When shall the vote be taken? Shall the provision for a vote be a part of the treaty? Is the cession dependent upon a favorable vote of the people?

Denmark contended that the vote should be taken after the treaty had been ratified by the Rigsdag. Mr. Seward began by refusing to have any vote whatever; after a while he consented to a vote before the Danish ratification. The Danes were strenuous on the point, and the Secretary finally yielded—agreeing to let them take it at their own pleasure. In fact, it was taken January 9, 1868—ten weeks after the treaty was signed, and more than a month after it was laid before our Senate.

Denmark contended that the provision for a vote should be a part of the treaty, and that the cession of the islands should be dependent upon the consent of the people. Her position was shown in the words of Count Frijs, on the 16th of June, as reported above by Mr. Yeaman. Mr. Seward took the opposite ground on both these questions.

The Danes wanted the provision for the vote in the treaty for the reason, as Mr. Yeaman wrote on the 22d of July, that it would embarrass their government "if the vote must be taken, to put itself in the attitude of negotiating a treaty positively, and then making its ratification depend upon a condition or event not provided for in the treaty." Of the conference of the 10th of August, Mr. Yeaman reported as follows:

"Count Frijs expressed his preference that, without agreeing in the treaty to submit the question of cession to a vote of the people of the islands, in such form as to make the vote decisive as a condition, yet to allude to it in such a manner as to show the fact of the intention of the government of Denmark to take the vote. I declined to agree to this, upon the ground that any such reference or statement in the treaty might be construed as an agreement to submit. He very much prefers its insertion and asked me if I would take it *ad referendum* which I agreed to do."

"We have reached a stage where failure would be positively painful," said Mr. Yeaman on the 5th of September, in a letter to Mr. Seward, advising him to yield some of the disputed points. The taking of the vote, he wrote on the 27th, they "deem a proper deference to modern European custom, and absolutely necessary in the present attitude of their other foreign relations." On the 28th, Mr. Seward wrote, in the pompous style often used in this correspondence, "we cannot now modify our previous instructions without putting the negotiations in great jeopardy."

On the 3d of October, Mr. Yeaman telegraphed:—"Denmark quite ready to conclude if vote mentioned in treaty." On the same day he wrote that he and Count Frijs had talked matters over—"he finds it necessary not only to ask the approbation of the people of the islands, but also equally necessary that their consent or approval should be referred to in the treaty, though not agreed upon as a condition precedent." On the following day Mr. Seward telegraphed, "no condition of vote in treaty." The very next day he changed his mind and telegraphed, "waive the objection and consent that a popular vote be taken in the islands at the instance of Denmark." That ended the matter, and in about two weeks thereafter the treaty was signed.

I recapitulate the positions of Mr. Seward that they may be seen at a glance. In May he thought a vote wholly unnecessary; in June he said Denmark might take a vote before ratification, but not after; in July he telegraphs that he will not agree to the vote at all; in August, by approving Mr. Yeaman's letter, he practically says that he will yield at the last moment and consent to a vote; in September he was against a vote and threatened to break off negotiations; on the 5th of October he executes his great *coup d'état* and yields everything at one stroke of the pen.

Could anything be much more humiliating to the nation than the showing which Mr. Seward has made for us in this St. Thomas correspondence? It is not worth while to throw hard words at him; the record he has made for himself is more severe for his condemnation than any language I could use. His way was a crooked way from first to last. He abused the confidence of the Danes, brought them into danger of a conflict with France, pledged our faith far beyond his warrant, put us into a false and embarrassing position before the civilized world. What shall we do to get out of this strait into which he has brought us? The question is one which Mr. Sumner's committee is considering.

DIXON.

HOW WE CARRIED THE ELECTION IN ST. THOMAS.

(FROM OUR REGULAR CORRESPONDENT.)

WASHINGTON, February 8, 1869.

On the 18th of last month I said that in this St. Thomas correspondence there was nothing more worthy our attention than the part relating to the vote of the people of the islands on the question of a transfer to the United States. In my letter of that date I showed you by what steps the contracting parties, Denmark and our Government, had reached an agreement on this point. I have just now come into possession of the documents bearing upon the work done in the islands, and am thus enabled to make the record complete. This I proceed to do, premising that there is nothing in it of which we have occasion to be proud.

The Danish government insisted from the first that a vote should be taken—"we shall require that the consent of the people of the islands shall be had," said Count Frijs on the 17th of May, 1867, when he consented to negotiate. From this position he was not moved.

Mr. Seward in that same May wrote, "it is not believed that the consent of the people of the islands is necessary." To this position he held till six months of negotiation had convinced him that the Danes would not yield—then, on the 5th of October, he telegraphed to Mr. Yeaman, "waive the objection, and consent that a popular vote be taken in the islands at the instance of Denmark."

When shall the vote be taken? was a question long in dispute. Count Frijs said, "after the ratification," in accordance with the precedent established when Nice and Savoy were ceded to France. The Danes held that this would leave our Senate and their Rigsdag free to act. Mr. Seward wrote, "consent is not given to await or depend upon the vote of the people of the islands." He seemed to fear that France and England would intrigue against us, and so defeat us in the popular vote. Letter after letter was written, argument after argument was advanced by Mr. Yeaman; the Danes declared that there must be a vote, that the taking of it must be mentioned in the treaty, and that the fate of the cession must be dependent upon the result. They finally carried their point—yielding so far as to consent that the vote might be taken before, rather than after, ratification.

The treaty was signed October 24, 1867. "I cherish the lively hope that what has been done at Copenhagen may be approved by the people of the islands, and by the President and the Senate," said Mr. Yeaman exuberantly on the following day in closing his long letter to Mr. Seward. Measures were at once taken by the Secretary to secure the approval of the islands.

The Rev. Charles Hawley, of Auburn, New York, and Rear-Admiral Palmer, with the Susquehanna, were sent down there "to coöperate with the Danish Commissioner," (Carstensen,) for the purpose of inducing the residents to vote for the transfer. Rev. Dr. Hawley's letter of appointment and instruction, dated October 26, 1867, two days after the treaty was signed, contained the following delicious paragraph:

"It is presumed that you will be at no loss for arguments to show, those who may have votes upon the subject the advantages which they would derive from transferring their allegiance to the United States, should they think proper to remain in the Islands. The market of this country, even now, is an eligible one for their products; and it must become much more so in the event of their annexation. As one of the purposes of this government in the acquisition is to secure a naval station, the inhabitants of the Islands will derive benefits from that which it is needless to expatiate upon. If, too, they should become a part of the domain of the United States, they and their posterity will have the same right to protection by a powerful government in war, and to those advantages in time of peace, which are enjoyed by other citizens."

"You will consider your attendance at St. Thomas as of a character entirely confidential," said Mr. Seward to Mr. Hawley. All the consuls, and consular agents, and naval officers of the United States in the islands were directed to use their influence with Mr. Hawley in securing a favorable vote. He reached St. Thomas on the 12th of November, and found Messrs Perkins and Moore, our consuls, and

Vice-Consul Simmons, already in the field. Two days thereafter he wrote to Mr. Seward:

"There is much inquiry whether the United States will continue St. Thomas a free port. If the merchants and others connected with the business relations of the island could be assured that there would be no change in this regard, and that their trade with the other islands would be maintained with its present advantages, the formidable objection to the transfer would be obviated. The whole issue, as they contemplate it, resolves itself into a question of trade."

The Danish Commissioner, Mr. Carstensen, reached St. Thomas on the 17th of November, and on the following day, with Mr. Hawley and Mr. Perkins, went over to St. Croix to see the Governor. Admiral Palmer, with his flagship, arrived at the same time. On the 22d, Mr. Hawley writes that he has talked a good deal with Mr. Carstensen, whom he found "unwilling to order an election until reasonably assured that the vote will be favorable." Our agent again alludes to the trade question—saying, in substance, that it would be easy to carry the vote if the people could be assured that "the present privileges and immunities enjoyed by the port will, for a time at least, remain undisturbed." This was the question on which the issue turned. How Mr. Hawley met it will appear from the reports:

"November 22, 1867.—I have said to those with whom I have talked that the principal design of the United States in acquiring these islands being the establishment of a naval depot, I had no doubt there would be as little change as possible in the present status of the port; and that our Government would be disposed to a liberal policy towards its new possessions, and retain to them all rights and immunities not in conflict with the common interest, besides the advantage they would have in the protection and privileges which a generous and powerful government accords to all it citizens."

"November 29, 1867.—We stated that as the object of the United States in the acquisition of the Islands respected naval convenience rather than revenue, there would be a strong disposition to deal generously with existing privileges, by appropriate legislation; and, moreover, if they would accept the manifest desire of Denmark to cede this territory to the United States, and leave their interests with us, their confidence would not be misplaced."

Two or three formal conferences were held, at which were present the Danish Commissioner, the Governor of the Islands, Messrs. Hawley, Perkins and Moore, and many leading citizens. Our agent and consuls reiterated the views expressed in Mr. Hawley's letters, saying they had every reason to believe that "the action of Congress would be in a spirit wholly friendly to the islands, and that their prosperity would be carefully fostered and guarded by our Government." The Governor and business men wanted something rather more definite on this head, and finally put into the form of three additional articles to the treaty the guarantees they would like to have the United States give. On the 1st of December Messrs. Caratensen and Hawley concluded to come to Washington and see what could be done in the premises—bearing the proposed articles, a strong tter from the Governor in support of them, and a numerously signed memorial to the same effect from merchants and business men.

The Danish Commissioner conferred freely with Mr. Seward, members of the Committee on Foreign Relations, several prominent members of Congress, and a number of other leading government officers. The treaty was before the Senate, its general provisions were known to everybody in the country, its most important article had been read in the House, and, so far as could be ascertained, there was no material objection to its ratification. Mr. Carstensen remained here nearly three weeks; the Senate took no hostile action on the treaty; neither Mr. Seward nor Mr. Summer's committee uttered a word of warning; he "was, on the contrary, cheered on by all with whom he had occasion to confer;" finally he returned to St. Thomas, convinced that we "meant business," and determined on taking the vote immediately.

On the 16th of December, while Mr. Carstensen was here, Mr. Seward wrote a long letter to Mr. Hawley, in which he announced that the proposed additional articles could not be adopted, spoke of "the benignant operation of self-government in the United States," of "the rights and interests of the inhabitants of the ceded islands," of "the high and broad guarantees for the protection of life, liberty, and property, which the Constitution of the United States affords," and closed by saying that "through these constitutional guarantees the habitants of the ceded islands would secure rights superior even to those which they have so long enjoyed as a colony under the protection of Denmark."

Mr. Carstensen called a meeting of the business men of St. Thomas on the 4th of January, 1868, at which these concluding words of Mr. Seward's letter were read as a pledge from the Government of the United States. They turned the scale. The election was held on the 9th. St. John cast a unanimous vote of 205 for the cession; the result in St. Thomas was 1,039 for and 22 against. And so, by Mr. Hawley's arguments, the presence of our fleet, the labors of Messrs. Perkins and Moore, the promises of Mr. Seward, and the inaction of Mr. Sumner's Committee and the Senate, the people of the islands despite the fears and anxieties of the business men and the superstition of the lower classes, dissolved their connection with Denmark and declared for a union with the United States.

That our people have been put in an embarrassing position by the action of Mr. Seward and the government, was revealed as soon as I began to examine the St. Thomas correspondence. Can the Senate show guiltless hands? A word from that body while Mr. Carstensen was here in December, 1867, a simple resolution of warning from the Committee on Foreign Relations, would have stopped the proceedings in the islands. That word was not uttered, that resolution was not offered: can the Senate throw stones at Mr. Seward's glass house? Have Mr. Seward, the President, the Cabinet, the Committee, and the Senate carried us so far that we must now ratify the treaty? If we reject it, will Denmark have a right to say before the world that she has found the United States wanting in both honor and justice? Mr. Sumner's committee is pondering this question. DIXON.

CAN THE ST. THOMAS TREATY BE REJECTED?

(FROM OUR REGULAR CORRESPONDENT.)

WASHINGTON, February 22, 1869.

It was in January, 1865, during the Presidency of Mr. Lincoln and the days of the Thirty-ninth Congress, that Mr. Seward opened negotiations for the purpose of the Danish West India Islands. It was in October, 1867, during the Presidency of Mr. Johnson and the days of the Fortieth Congress, that a treaty was concluded. It will be in 1869, during the Presidency of Mr. Grant and the days of the Forty-first Congress, when we take final action upon the treaty.

Six weeks ago I began looking into the matter of the long negotiation, hoping nothing more than to find the material for one or two readable letters to the *Daily Advertiser*. I write now as one of those whom the present Senate and the present Administration have compromised—as one of the great body of citizens whose rights must be considered when the new Senate of the next Congress makes up its decision.

The United States is a great power and Denmark is a small power. If our positions were reversed—if we were the small State and Denmark were the great State—I feel sure that every man of us conversant with the facts would think himself wronged if Denmark were to treat the United States as we have treated Denmark. We are strong enough to conquer any armed foe within or without: I trust the final event will show that we are strong enough to love honor and justice.

The Danes had no wish to sell their islands—they did not ask us to buy them as Russia asked us to buy Alaska. Mr. Seward's urgency in the matter; his temptation, through Mr. Yeaman, of an alliance with the United States; his special mission of the summer of 1868, through Senator Doolittle, to the Danish Government; the general support given by our people to his foreign policy; the ratification of the Alaska purchase almost without objection—these were the things that led the Danes into the making of the St. Thomas treaty.

The way of Mr. Seward was, as I have already said, a crooked way. The Danish cabinet, when it formally consented to negotiate, asked that the treaty, if made, should first be ratified by the Rigsdag, then by the islands, finally by the United States. The Secretary for a long time refused to submit the matter to the islands at all, but finally consented to let them vote upon the treaty before it was taken up by the Rigsdag. The Danes disliked this proposition. To them it was a yielding of the whole question—Count Frijs told Mr. Yeaman, as appears from a letter in the State Department, that Denmark would consider herself fully committed to the treaty by a favorable vote of St. Thomas and San Juan. But Mr. Seward at last carried his point—in my letter of two weeks ago I showed by what means we secured the affirmative voice of the islands. He said, in one of his letters, that the taking of the vote was none of our concern, but an act of Denmark for her own satisfaction—still he had interest enough in the business to send Rev. Dr. Hawley down, to instruct our consuls in the premises, and to bring Admiral Palmer and his flag-ship into the harbor. The people were at first decidedly opposed to annexation but Mr. Seward's assurance that through it "the inhabitants of the ceded islands would secure rights superior even to those which they have so long enjoyed as a colony under the protection of Denmark,' induced them to consent. This consent Denmark regarded as a pledge that she would ratify the treaty; and, after action by the Rigsdag, it was signed by the King, on the 31st of January, 1868, in ample time for the exchange of ratifications, which exchange was to have taken place here on or before February 24th of that year. Denmark did everything in a prompt and honorable manner on her part to give effect to the treaty. Now let me show what Mr. Seward did after he had got her irrevocably committed thereto through the result of the vote in the islands.

In the last days of 1867 or the first days of 1868—before the people of the islands had voted—an agent of the Government of San Domingo reached here with authority to negotiate about Samana. Mark the date—*before* the vote was had in St. Thomas, and while the Danish Commissioner and Dr. Hawley were up here to see how things looked and to get Mr. Seward's assurance of "rights superior." The Secretary kept his own counsel—as soon as Hawley and Carstensen were gone he made a basis for treating with San Domingo, sent it to the Committee on Foreign Relations, then went before that committee for a talk, and *gave its members the impression that he did not want the St. Thomas treaty ratified* because he thought he might drive a better bargain for Samana. What must Denmark think of this as an illustration of the "liberal and chivalrous spirit" of dealing to which Mr. Seward, in January, 1865, pledged the United States?

The way of the Senate was not an honorable way—indeed, it wa a way the United States cannot afford to have any future Senate take.s It received the Danish treaty from the President early in the session of 1867–68. The Government of Denmark knew, all the while, that action upon the document was required at the hands of this body. It had a right to ask that this action be taken within the time named in the treaty itself. Yet in all the twelves weeks, from December 3, 1867, to February 24, 1868, nothing was done. The Danish Commissioner and Rev. Dr. Hawley came here the first week in December and remained two or three weeks. The Committee on Foreign Relations, which had the matter in charge, might properly enough have acted during their visit; if the islands were not wanted, we could have said so at once, and thus have made an end of the whole business. The committee said nothing; did not even hint its purpose of inaction. Mr. Seward went before it and gave his views about Samana, and still there was no action. February came, and the committee, with time and inclination to attend to everything else, could find no day in which to pass upon this issue. At that period, a year ago, prior to the day fixed for the exchange of ratifications, the treaty might, perhaps, in spite of Mr. Seward's crooked course in the negotiation, have been rejected without discredit to the country. Denmark would probably have regretted its rejection, but there could hardly have been any serious complaint against the United States as a nation; for while the Executive had a clear right to negotiate the treaty, the Senate had an equally clear right to reject it. February went by, and then followed the months to July, in the end of which Congress adjourned. The Senate had not passed upon the question of ratification—even Mr. Sumner's committee had not passed upon it.

An additional article was soon afterward signed, extending the time for the exchange of ratifications to October of this year Congress met again in December, three months ago, and when the holiday adjournment took place this St. Thomas document had not yet been touched. I need not assert that the course of the Senate with respect to the treaty was discreditable—the statement of facts is in itself enough. Mr. Sumner's committee held the convention for nine months, neither saying anything nor doing anything; and no member of the body called for a report on the question it had been charged to consider. The way of this committee and this Senate is a way we have a right to demand shall never again be followed.

Six or seven weeks ago General Raasloff arrived here. He was the Danish Minister in this country when the St. Thomas negotiations began; at their close he was, as he is now, the Danish Minister of War in the home government. He is here to close up the business in some way. It is not creditable to us that the causeless delay of the Senate should force Denmark to send him, or any one else, as a special messenger to ask action upon the treaty—this thing is not creditable to the United States. When he arrived the convention lay in one of the pigeon-holes of Mr. Sumner's committee, where it had been quietly lying for a year. One thing he has accomplished: he has compelled the committee to take it up and consider it on its merits. So much has been gained, and, in view of the past, this is a good deal. But a better thing yet has been accomplished—he has roused the attention of the country to the matter, so that the treaty is no longer a dead parchment, but a living thing asking a question that we must soon answer. That question is, ratify, or reject?

The new administration will bring in a new order of things. I find that when persons are asked to look at this St. Thomas purchase, they can mostly see nothing but Mr. Seward, for whom there is of late not much love. He will soon be out of the way—then we ought to be able to determine what is fair and equitable. Do we want St. Thomas, and is it worth the money we have bargained to give? Answer these questions affirmatively, and there is no need to speak further. For my part, I am satisfied that it would be far better to pay seven and a half millions for St. Thomas and San Juan than take Samana and the whole of St. Domingo as a gift. There are some presents that a nation cannot afford to accept, and St. Domingo and its people are one of these. Have Mr. Seward and the Senate so involved us that honor and justice alike require us to ratify this treaty? The new President, the new Secretary of State, and the Senate in the next Congress, must consider this question. It raises an issue which the country cannot wisely ignore. Denmark is a small power; but the answer we make will be heard through the civilized world.

DIXON.

APPENDIX.

THE TEXT OF THE TREATY.

Convention between His Majesty the King of Denmark,

and

the united states of america,

Concerning the cession of the Islands of St. Thomas and St. John in the West Indies.

His Majesty the King of Denmark and the United States of America being desirous of confirming the good understanding which exists between them, have for that purpose appointed as Plenipotentiaries, his Majesty the King of Denmark, Count Christian Emil Juel Vind-Frijs, President of the Council of the Ministers and Minister for Foreign Affairs, Grandcross of the Order of Danebrog, and decorated with the Cross of honor of the same Order, and the President of the United States, George H. Yeaman, accredited as their Minister Resident to his said Majesty, and the said Plenipotentiaries having exchanged their full powers, which were found to be in due form, have agreed upon and signed the following articles:

Article I.

His Majesty the King of Denmark agrees to cede to the United States by this Convention immediately upon the exchange of the ratifications thereof, the islands of St. Thomas and St. John in the West Indies, with the adjacent islands and rocks, situated north of the 18th degree of north latitude.

His Majesty the King of Denmark will, however, not exercise any constraint over the people, and will, therefore, as soon as practicable, give them an opportunity of freely expressing their wishes in regard to this cession.

ARTICLE II.

In the cession of territory and dominion made by the preceding article are included the right of property of the crown of Denmark in all public lots and squares, vacant lands, and all public buildings, fortifications, barracks and other edifices which are not private individual property. It is, however, understood that the Lutheran Congregations shall remain in possession of the churches which are now used by them, and that sums due the Danish treasury by individuals are reserved and do not pass by this cession.

Any government archives, papers and documents relative to the territory and dominion aforesaid, which may be now existing there, shall be left in the possession of the agent of the United States appointed in accordance with Article IV, but an authenticated copy of such of them as may be required will be at all times given by the United States to the Danish Government, or to such Danish officers or subjects as may apply to them.

ARTICLE III.

The inhabitants of the said islands shall be protected in their liberty, their religion, their property and private rights, and they shall be free to remain where they now reside, or to remove at any time, retaining the property which they possess in the said islands, or disposing thereof and removing the proceeds wherever they please, without their being subjected on this account to any contribution, tax or charge whatever. Those who shall prefer to remain in the said islands, may either retain the title and the right of their natural allegiance, or acquire those of citizens of the United States. But they shall make their election within two years from the date of the exchange of ratifications of this convention; and those who shall remain in the said islands after the expiration of that terms, without having declared their intention to retain their natural allegiance, shall be considered to have elected to become citizens of the United States.

ARTICLE IV.

Immediately after the payment by the United States of the sum of money stipulated for in the fifth article of this Convention, His Majesty the King of Denmark will appoint an agent or agents for the purpose of formally delivering to a similar agent or agents, appointed on behalf of the United States, the territory, islands, property and appurtenances which are ceded as above, including any fortifications or military posts which may be in the ceded territory, and for doing any other act which may be necessary in regard thereto. But the cession with the right of immediate possession is nevertheless to be deemed complete and absolute on the exchange of ratifications, without waiting for such formal delivery. Any Danish troops, which may be in the territory or aforesaid islands, shall be withdrawn as soon as may be reasonably and conveniently practicable.

Article V.

In consideration of the cession aforesaid, the United States agree to pay, at the treasury in Washington, within three months after the exchange of the ratifications of this convention, to the diplomatic representative or other agent of His Majesty the King of Denmark, duly authorized to receive the same, seven millions five hundred thousand dollars, in gold.

The cession conveys to the United States the said islands and appurtenances in full and entire sovereignty, with all the dominion, rights and powers which Denmark now possesses and can exercise in them, free and unincumbered by any grants, conditions, privileges or franchises in any way affecting or limiting the exercise of such sovereignty.

Article VI.

When this convention shall have been duly ratified by His Majesty the King of Denmark, by and with the consent of the Rigsdag on the one part, and on the other by the President of the United States, by and with the advice and consent of the Senate, the ratifications shall be exchanged at Washington, within four months from the date hereof, or sooner if possible.

In faith whereof the respective Plenipotentiaries have signed this convention and thereto affixed the seals of their arms.

Done at Copenhagen, the 24th of October, in the year of our Lord one thousand eight hundred and sixty-seven.

Geo. H. Yeaman, [L. S.]
C. E. Juel-Vind-Frijs, [L. S.]

www.ingramcontent.com/pod-product-compliance
Lightning Source LLC
LaVergne TN
LVHW011145110826
845150LV00008B/2519
* 9 7 8 1 4 1 8 1 9 2 4 7 1 *